Early American Embroidery Designs

An 1815 Manuscript Album with Over 190 Patterns

by

Elizabeth M. Townshend

Dover Publications, Inc.
New York

Copyright © 1985 by Dover Publications, Inc.
All rights reserved under Pan American and International
Copyright Conventions.

Published in Canada by General Publishing Company, Ltd.,
30 Lesmill Road, Don Mills, Toronto, Ontario.
Published in the United Kingdom by Constable and Company, Ltd.,
10 Orange Street, London WC2H 7EG.

*Early American Embroidery Designs: An 1815 Manuscript Album
with Over 190 Patterns* is a new work,
first published by Dover Publications, Inc., in 1985.
It is the first publication of an original hand-drawn album.

Manufactured in the United States of America
Dover Publications, Inc.,
31 East 2nd Street, Mineola, N.Y. 11501.

Library of Congress Cataloging in Publication Data

Townshend, Elizabeth M.
Early American embroidery designs.

(Dover needlework series)
1. Embroidery—United States—History—19th century—
Themes, motives. I. Title. II. Series.
NK9212.T68 1985   746.44   85-16066
ISBN 0-486-24946-8 (pbk.)

Publisher's Note

This book reproduces in its entirety a hand-drawn album signed and dated 1815 by Elizabeth M. Townshend. Although we have no information about the artist, the drawings appear to be patterns for embroidery; several of them seem to have no application except as designs for embroidered edgings. Such hand-drawn pattern books were common in the eighteenth and nineteenth centuries, but few of them have survived to the present. The most common method of transferring the designs to fabric involved pricking the lines of the pattern with a pin, placing the pattern over the fabric and sifting powdered charcoal through the holes. Not surprisingly, the patterns eventually fell to pieces. Why Elizabeth Townshend's patterns were never pricked and have thus survived, we don't know. Perhaps her tastes ran more to the creation or rendering of designs than to their actual execution with the needle. But there is another possibility:

Embroidery was an extremely popular pastime for women in the eighteenth and nineteenth centuries. All women learned "plain" sewing for making basic clothing and for mending, but decorative stitching, or "fancywork," was done primarily by the well-to-do who had the leisure time to devote to it. Fine embroidery was the hallmark of a lady, and no gentlewoman's education was complete until she could demonstrate her skill with the needle. Numerous schools were established to teach young ladies the genteel art of embroidery, and early in America's history we find records of such "female academies" being opened. The Revolutionary War interrupted the operation of these schools, but by the close of the eighteenth century, such academies were once again flourishing. It is very possible that Elizabeth Townshend attended one of these schools and made these drawings while a pupil there. Drawing and

painting, as well as embroidery, were taught, and the book could well have served as a combination exercise book for drawing classes and an embroidery pattern book (without the necessity of execution of the needlework). Rudimentary botany may well have been taught at Elizabeth's school, as it was at many others, for many of the flowers and leaves in her drawings are done with some degree of realism. In addition to devising their own designs, students may have been set to copying designs from one of the many books of embroidery patterns available at the time. While these books were not as common in America as in England and Europe, it is likely that most of the academies possessed a copy of at least one such book and used it in their teaching.

The designs in the book range from highly stylized repeat patterns, to more realistic floral bouquets, to patterns for cutwork edgings, to large-scale motifs suitable for crewel embroidery. In the United States, crewel work was beginning to fade in popularity by the beginning of the nineteenth century. Embroidery with wool, while not completely abandoned, was giving way to embroidery using finer silk threads. Most of Elizabeth's designs are relatively small in scale and appear to have been planned for use with silk threads. A few, however, such as the floral in the center of page 3, the vine at the left on page 18 and the two large designs on page 39, would be particularly effective worked in wool. Cutwork was also popular during this period, often worked entirely in white to edge fine bed linens and undergarments. Many of the designs shown here, such as those on pages 32 and 40, appear to illustrate such cutwork edgings. The majority of drawings in the book are repeat patterns, designed either for edgings or for bands of pattern. However, the large floral motifs on pages 15 and 16 and the tiny florals on page 34 were meant to be used singly. Baskets were a popular motif of the day and the miniature baskets on page 33 are particularly charming spot designs. The dainty little leaf pattern at the upper right of page 20 is an example of an allover pattern, planned perhaps for a waistcoat or petticoat. We don't know what Elizabeth had in mind when she drew the large curved design on page 42, but some possibilities are decorating a fan or embellishing the collar or cuffs of a favorite dress.

The stitches that Elizabeth would have used to execute these designs are the same stitches that we use today. Crewel work made extensive use of long-and-short stitch, seed stitch, outline and stem stitches, chain stitch, loop stitch and herringbone stitch. Satin stitch was also used, but the Roumanian stitch was preferred for covering large areas because it was longer-wearing and more economical of thread than satin stitch. Embroidery in America tended to be simpler than its English or European counterpart, using fewer kinds of stitches in a given piece. Some superb examples of Early American embroidery use only three or four different stitches to achieve their effect. For example, the vine on the left of page 39 could have been effectively worked by filling the berries with spirals of chain stitch, using chain or stem stitch for the stem and working the leaves in herringbone stitch. Embroidery with silk used many of the same simple stitches as crewel. The second design from the top on page 6 could have been worked with outline stitch stems, detached chain stitch (also known as lazy daisy stitch) leaves and seed stitch dots. The basic stitch used in cutwork was a close buttonhole stitch, with woven fillings used to give interest to the eyelet openings. Several of Elizabeth's designs, such as the edging on the right of page 13, indicate such fillings.

Elizabeth Townshend's book is valuable not only for its historic interest but also as a source of designs for today's embroidery enthusiast. Most current books of Early American designs are compilations of patterns adapted from various media and thus altered in some way. These designs are completely authentic, coming to us straight from the pen of the artist who drew them.

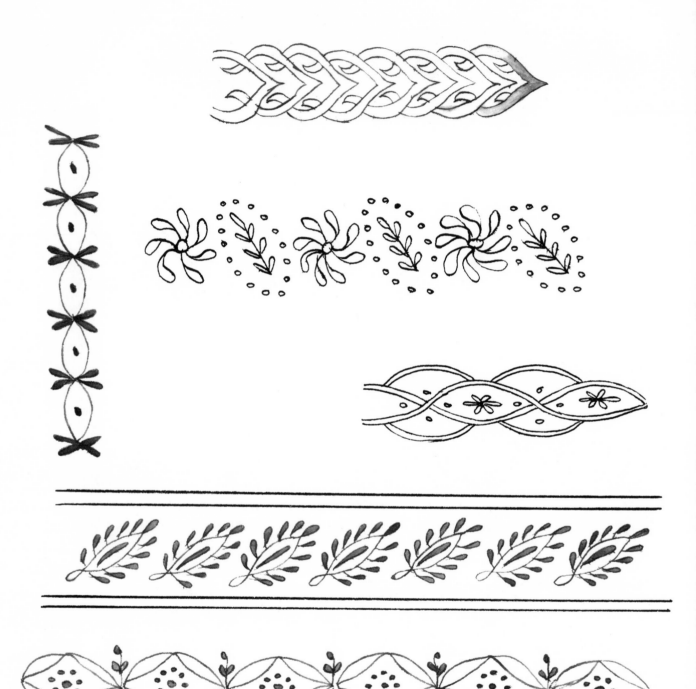

3

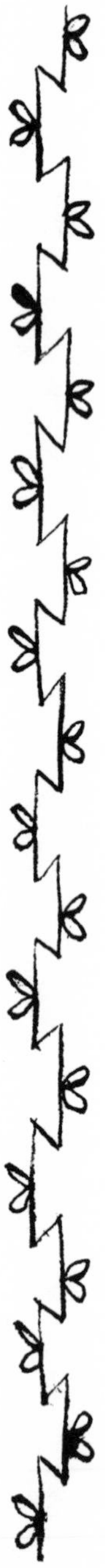

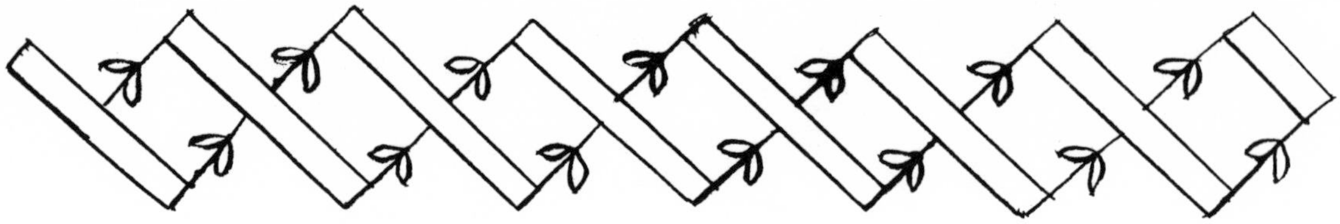

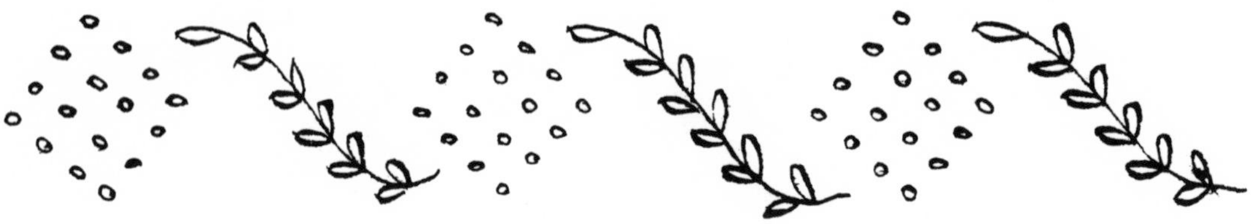

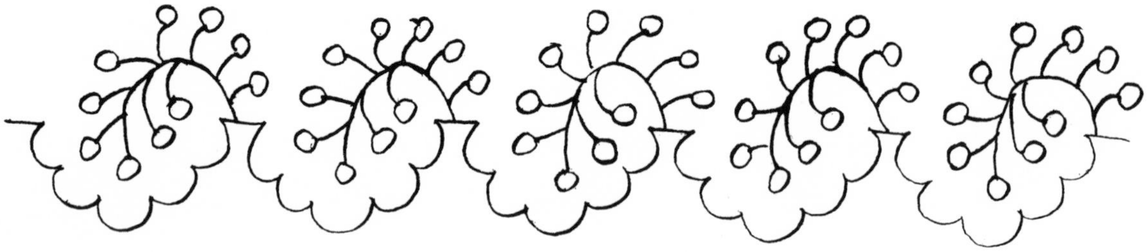

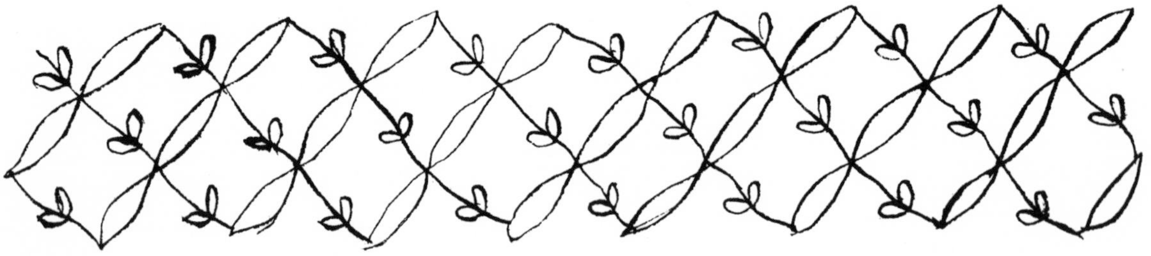

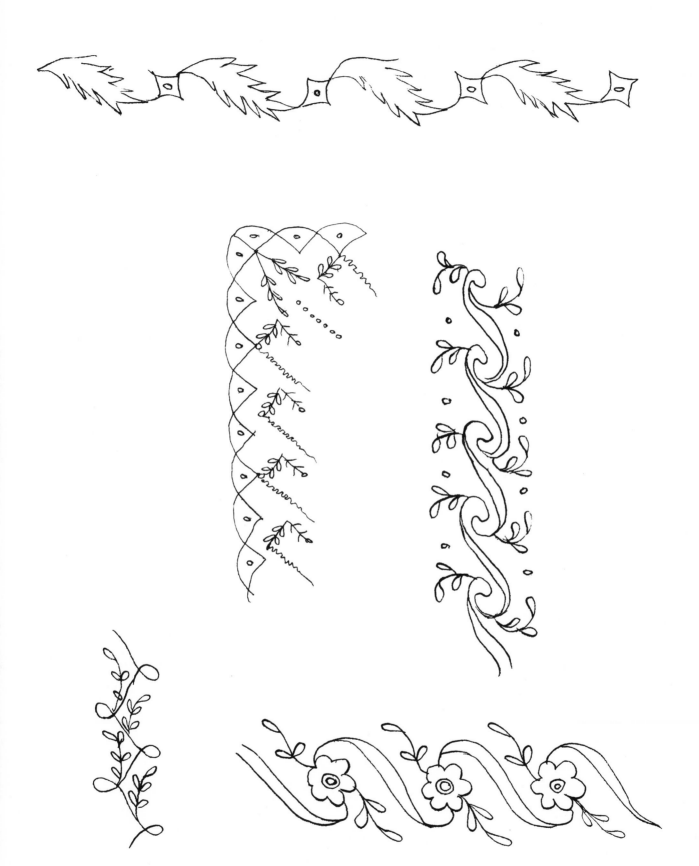

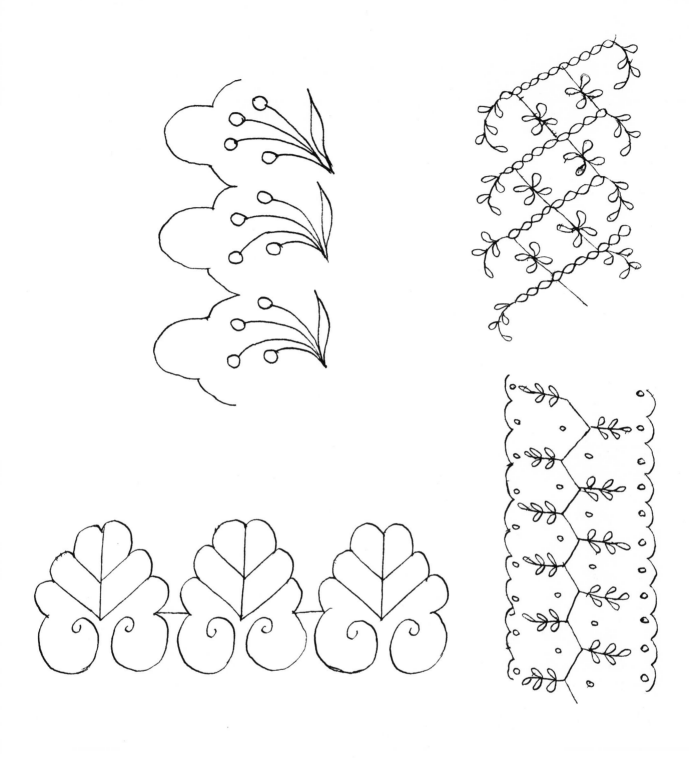

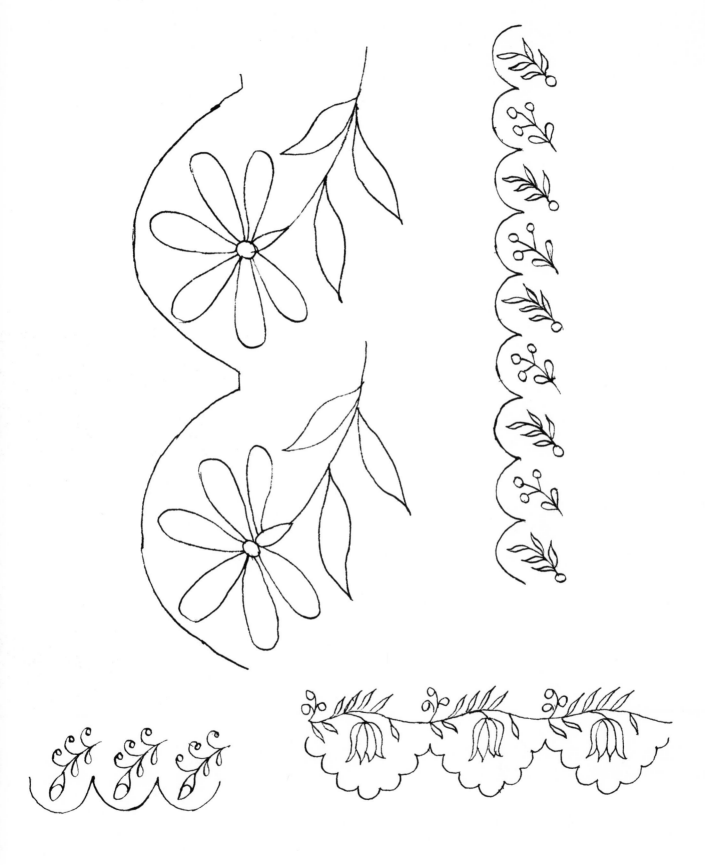

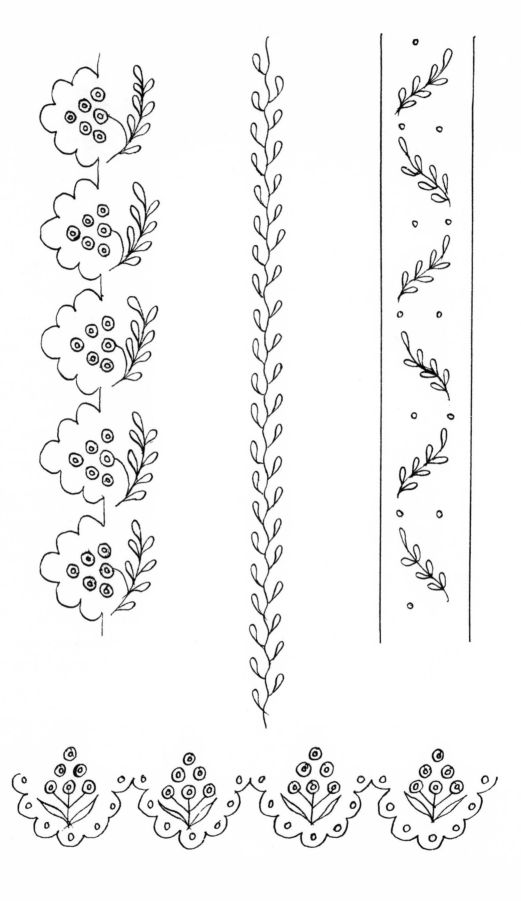

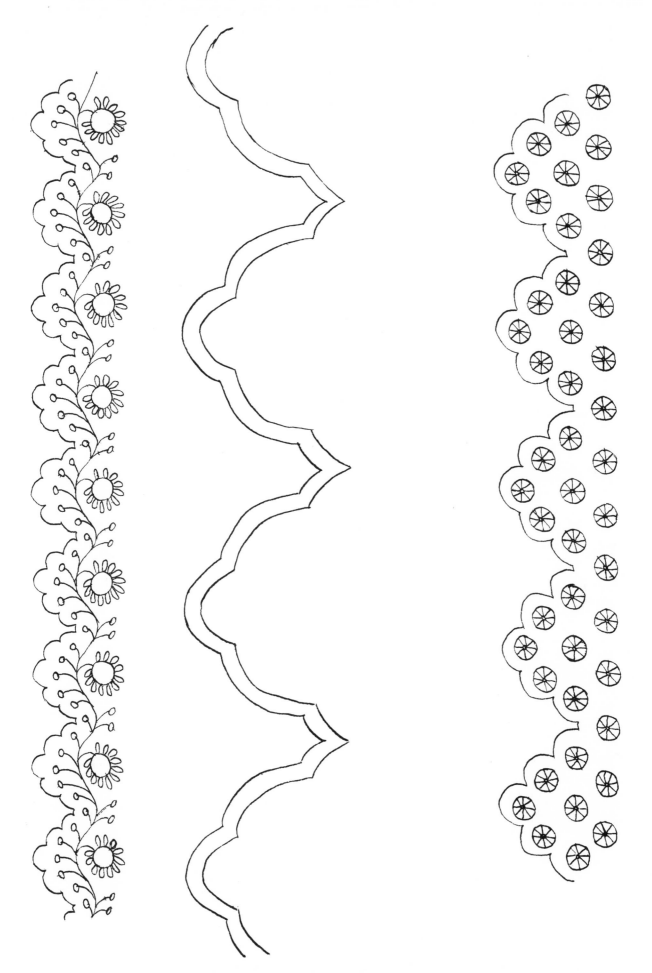

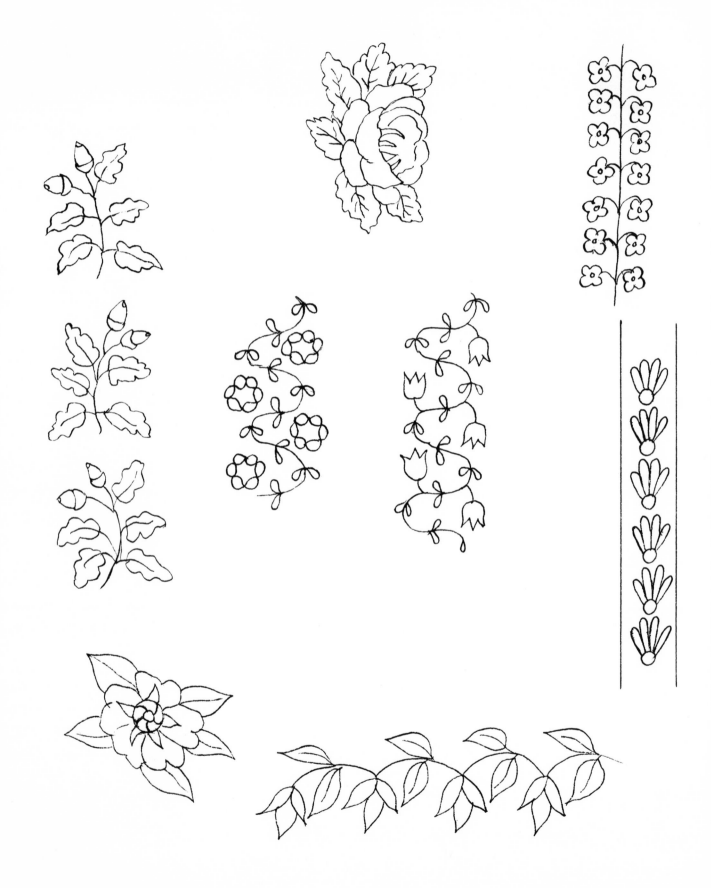

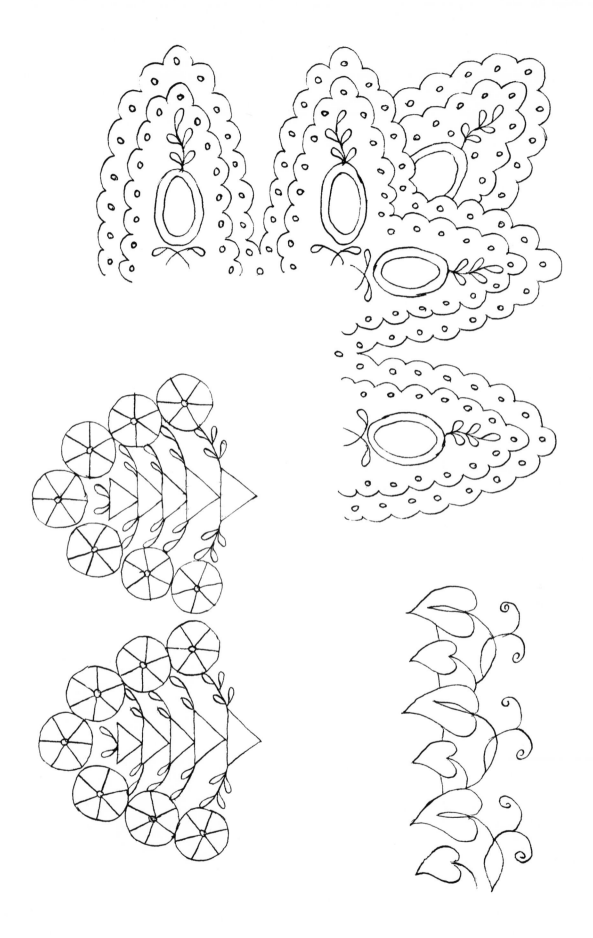

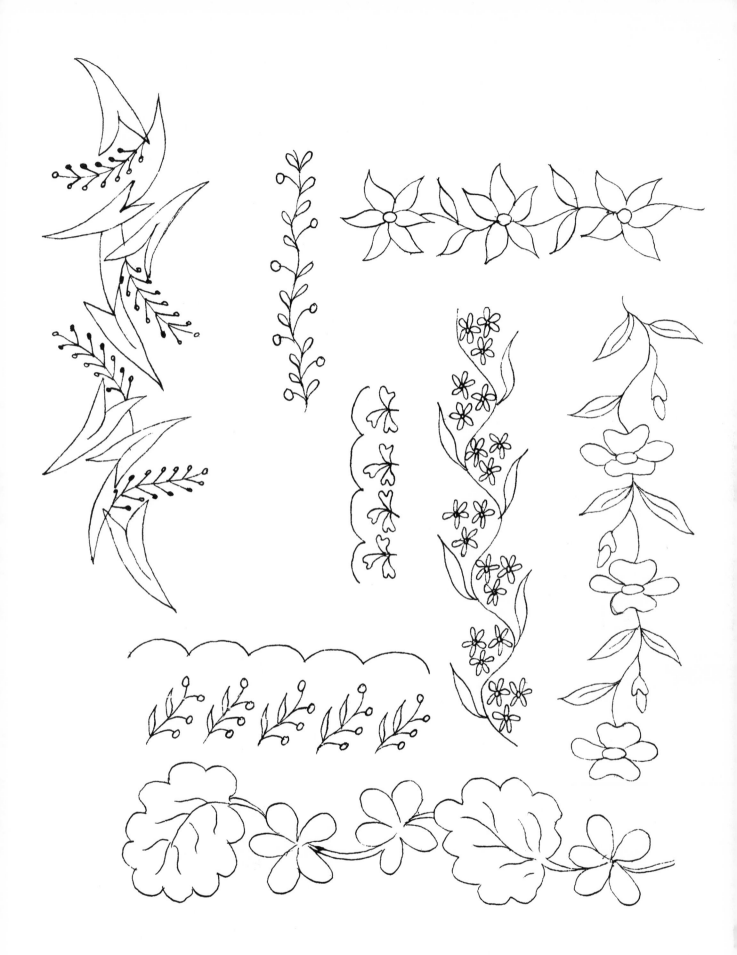

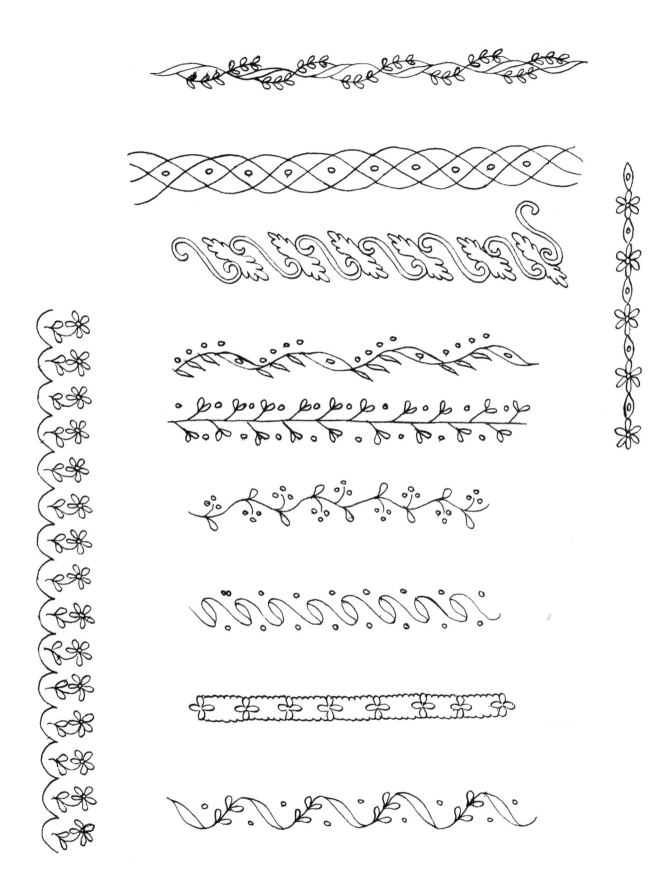

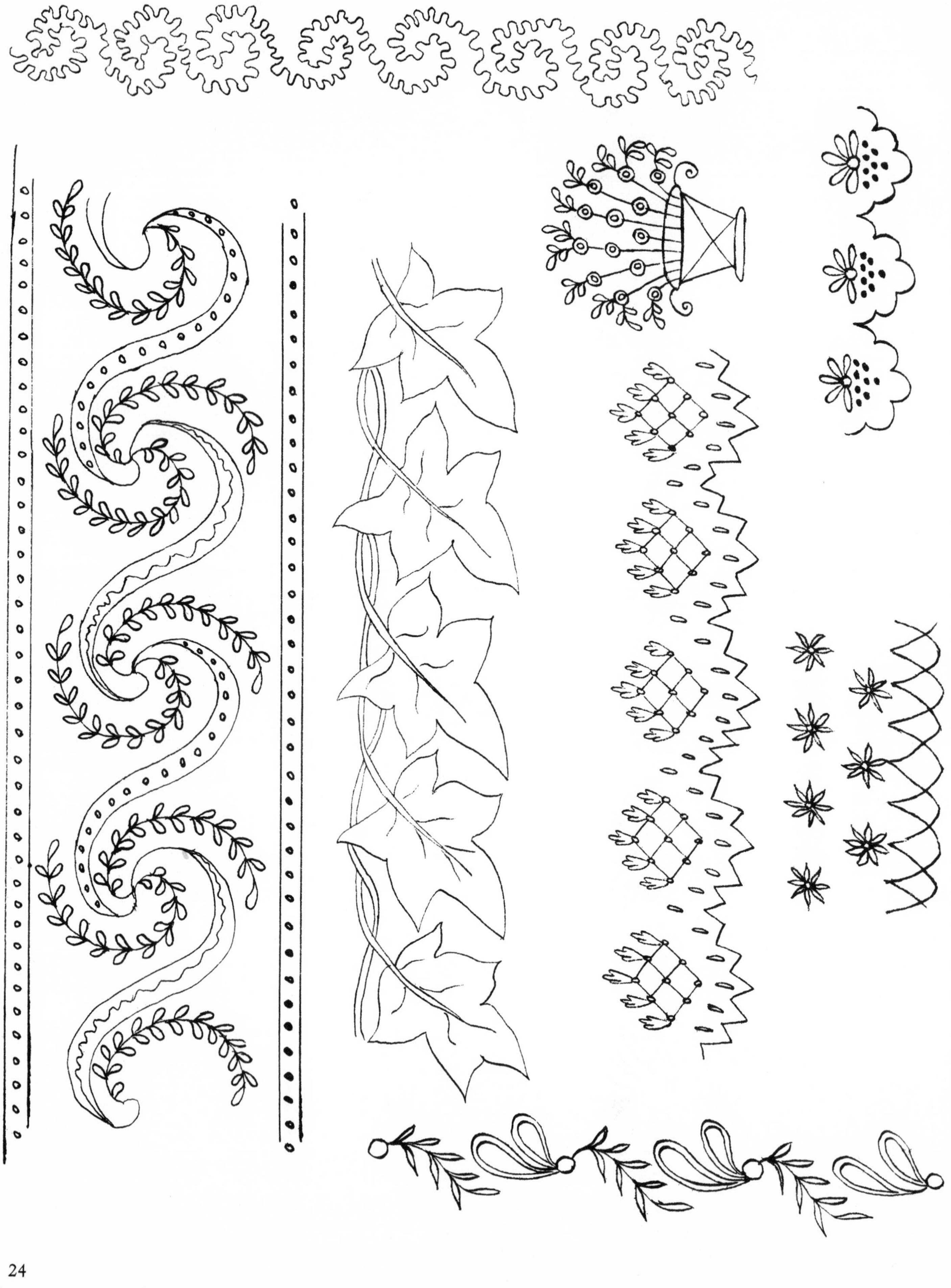

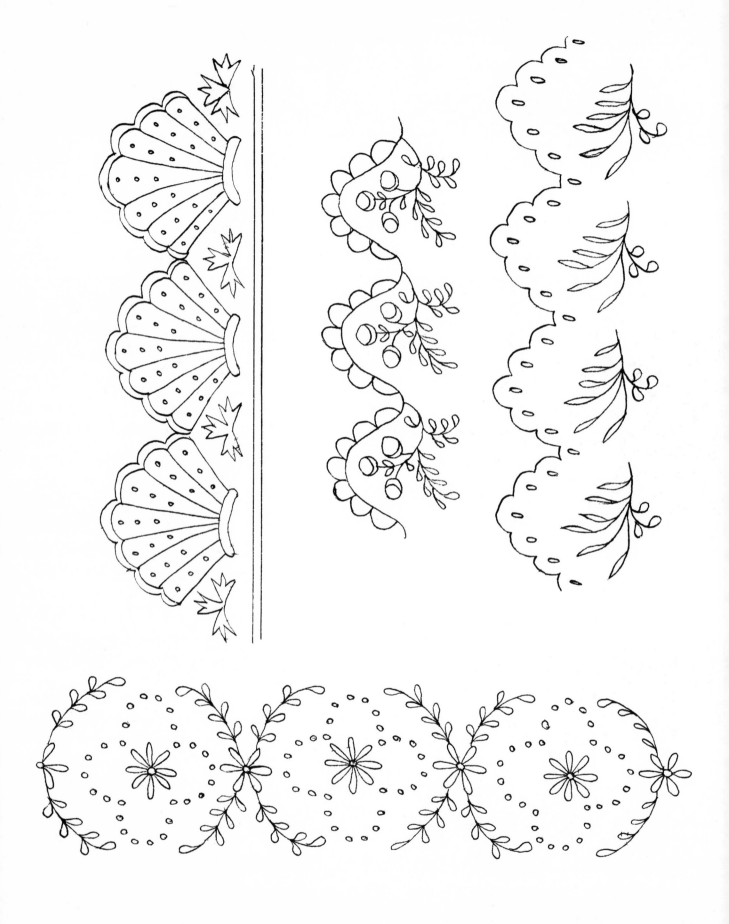

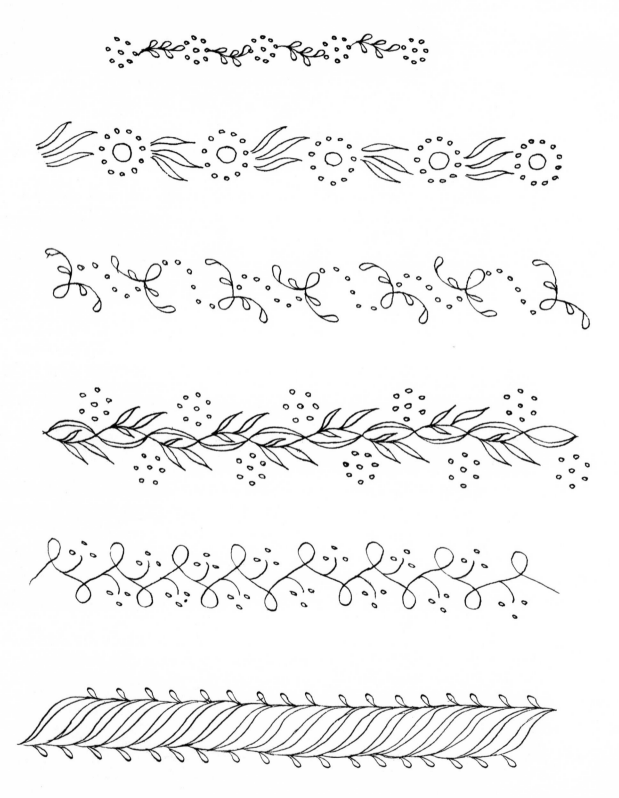

29

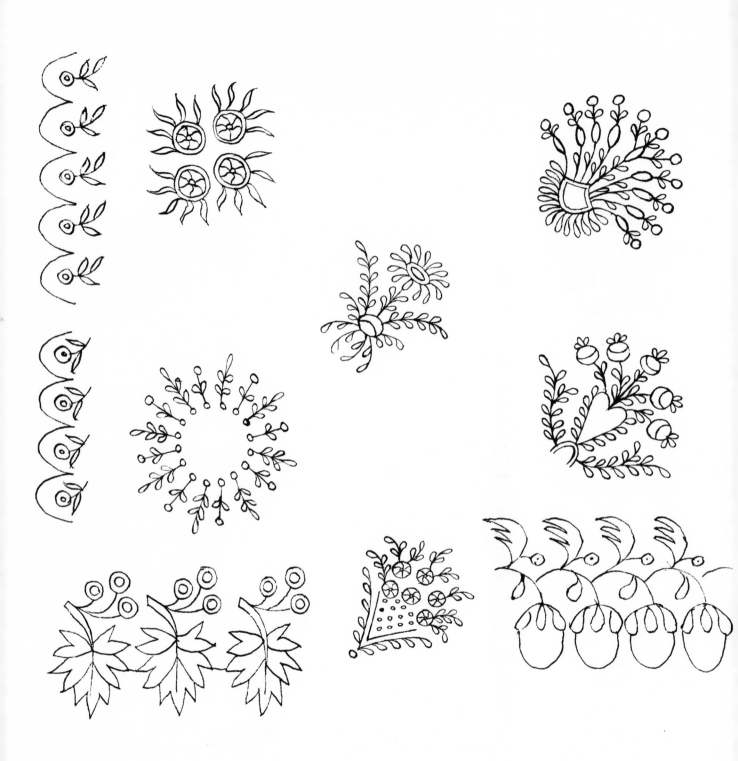

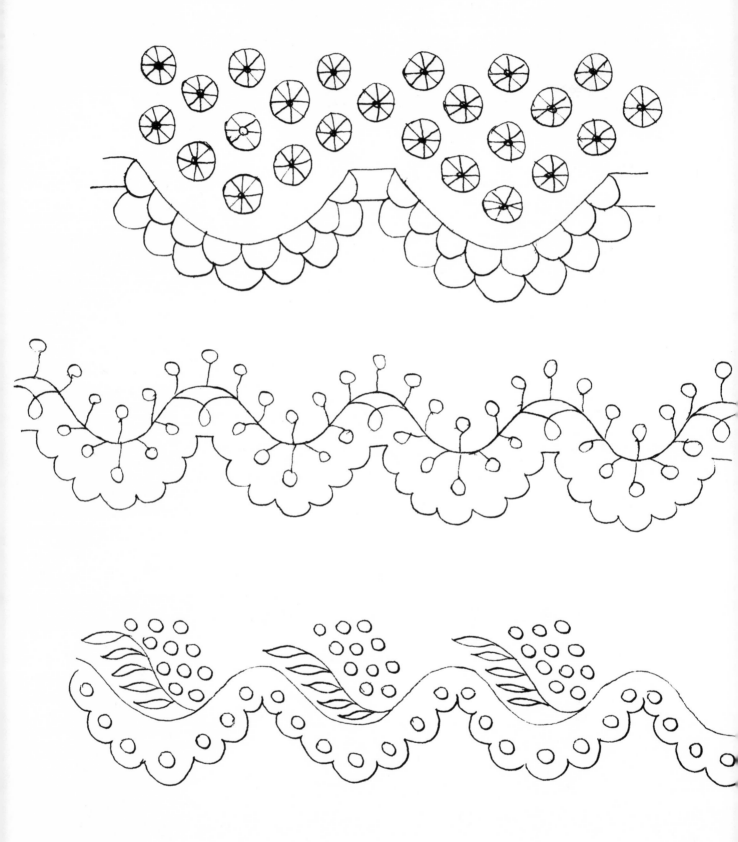

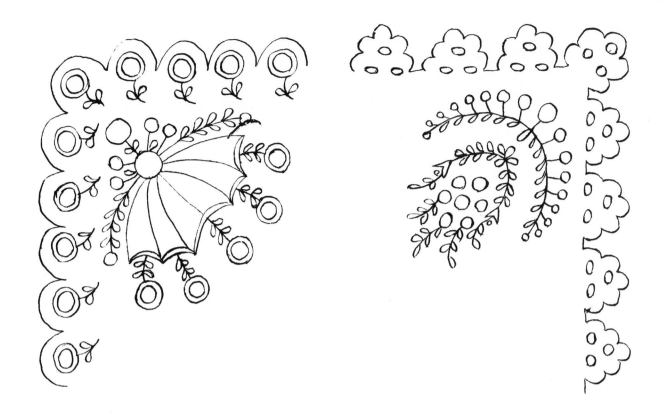

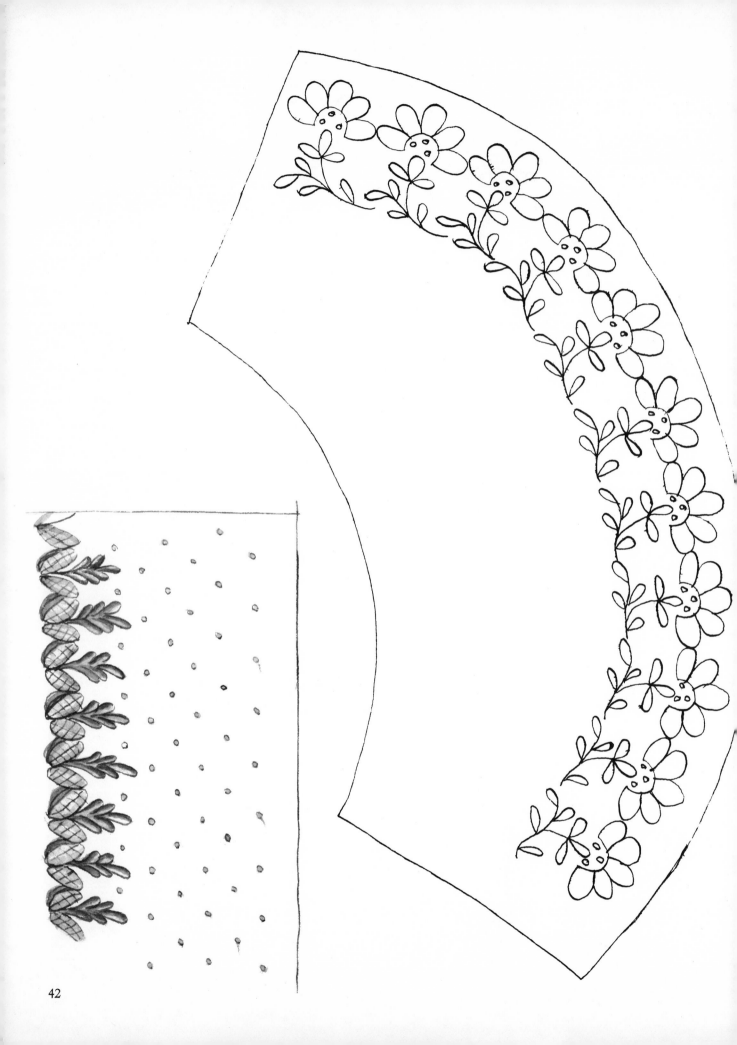